I0156812

fire lily:
flower of the flame

Nicolette van der Walt

fire lily: flower of the flame
Copyright © 2007 by Nicolette van der Walt

All rights reserved. No part of this book may be used or reproduced by any means, graphic, electronic or mechanical, including photocopying, recording, taping or by any information storage retrieval system without the written permission of the publisher except in the case of brief quotations embodied in critical articles and reviews.

ISBN: 978-0-6151-8143-1

First Edition

Contact the author:

P O Box 172
Mossel Bay
6500
Republic of South Africa
nicolettevdw@absamail.co.za

Cover Photograph: Dance Nude © Neotakezo / www.dreamstime.com
Cover Design: www.zayrayves.com

Published by: Magdalena & Co., Santa Clara, CA

Magdalena & Co.
Santa Clara, CA

Love is life.
All, everything that I understand,
I only understand because I love.

~ Leo Tolstoy

Acknowledgements:

The author wishes to thank the editors of the following publications where some of the poems in *Fire Lily: Flower of the Flame* were previously published or released on film:

Eyes of the Poet; Brother, My Cup; Float Like A Butterfly, Sing Like A Tree ... and other Poems; Dream Book of Dreams; as die son kom oogknip; Surrendering Thoughts – An Anthology of Verse; Allpoetry 1st Book Project; Wolanani – We embrace each other.

The author would like to thank Zayra Yves for her encouragement, generosity and amazing creative spirit along the journey to the publication of this book as well as for promoting it and also for dedicating her audio CD *Sleep in the Sea Tonight with Me* to the author and to social workers worldwide. She also offers deep appreciation and love, both on a personal and professional level, to the following people for their inspiration, contributions, love and support towards work that appear in this book: Her three children, her parents, brother, sisters and their families, friends & colleagues, Steve Melvin, Wanda Brayton, Robin Maples, Karen Harris, Rob Ganson, Brian Douthit, Marc Creamore, Yossi (Joe) Faybish, Mary Kerkes and Zayra Yves. These people, as well as many others, were all key in her continued efforts in the expression of living life from the heart in love, passion and compassion.

to my children – Barend, Diane & Arnold,
and the "bokkie buoy"
~ with love, always

CONTENTS:

I. at the edge of the petal

II. hours of flower and flame

to poem this piano
quicksilver
poem for my heart
to put myself away
ever woman, ever growth
verse in largo
when all our doves leave us
from eve's diary
footnotes from a mother
sing
and when I close my eyes
promise you'll never think of me

III. your name in my mouth

in the saffron of our laughter
at peggy's cove
knowledge
blue pause
berceuse
how I see you (poem by quietly burning)
to pour myself as moon
touch, almost
of all my soft blue days
ache
wind
at 5:30 am
i hold your name in my mouth
eyes of the poet
whisper
at 6:00 am
and like the aromatic trees
the madness
pianissimo
new dress
flame

IV. a bite out of the moon

morning comes in amber
gingered
naked nights
para siempre
chanson
beached
dunes
fire damage
alliteration(s)
a vermilion hour
a lighter weight
we are so much lighter now
flame
anchored
daily bread
far, above
to cloud the sun
vibrato
on reading cummings
tambourine

V. of leaves and longing

facing a new day
i miss you like the leaves
like wind through a flute
weighted
slow lament
here my voice stumbles
quartered
opened
a lesson in winter
lost echo

when words escape
to window
too white the day
between your thoughts & your hands
september poem
seasons
when at night you embrace nothing
wind sleeve

VI. cluster of bright beads

to a child
voiceless
waiting for a poem
paternoster
siyabona africa!
ring of roses
namib
wolanani
nightfall
south africa: the long walk
here be dragons
small protest
living words
a poet

Introduction by Zayra Yves

In this passionate collection of poetry Nicolette van der Walt shares with her readers the intimacy of her very marrow. It more than a poet who shares their heart and soul through the beauty of flowers or the tragedy of their short lives, with Nicolette it is depth of love as it smolders within long after the fire has grown cool; her poetry is a window into longing that is more intense than mere desire.

It is an understatement to write that Nicolette is a master of the short form in poetry, as she clearly demonstrates in this collection that she is weightless but not lacking in brevity as she travels through the starless and moonless nights of deep pain. Then by turns of sunlight and flowers, she is every season of the earth as she guides her readers into unblinking truths that are as luminous in the dance of sublime understanding of love and loss, as they are of intimacy, lust, parenting, nature, society and celebrations.

Nicolette's is a woman of many gifts and strengths but of all those wonders, what stands out most is her grace. She is truly as graceful as a flower, as sensuous as a dancer and as passionate as the fire; she is what she writes. The poet and the poem are one as they dance together on the page from the seed of what is intensely personal and private to the core of all humanity burning with it the powerful yearning for union with the beloved. The rapture of her poetry will light a candle of beauty in your soul and open your heart to burn beyond the flame.

Zayra Yves
San Francisco, California 2007
www.zayrayves.com

*If seeds in the black earth
can turn into such beautiful flowers,
what might not the heart of man become
in its long journey toward the stars?*

~ *G.K. Chesterton*

at the edge of the petal

flowers are
love's truest language

~ Park Benjamin

vase

on the table a glass vase
fills with dawn: daffodil,

corn flower, poppy and a few rays
of anemone. I recall
mornings

when there were more
long-stemmed
colours

than my heart
could hold

daisy

a single ray fell from the sun,
settled on the *t* of two yellow-
wood floor boards. I wonder,
is it the returning *not* – or
perhaps a soft, white nod?

calla lily

the stalk a hand
that should be yours

and my breasts
not the silk route
of your mouth

I fall from my eyes
into this whirling
whiteness,

into yearning's
slow yellow
        exclamation

as tulips do

the tulip doesn't know the word pink,
but lives it every day, warm
as the inside of a mouth

its petals don't know their name
but the inner-breath of lovers
repeats it over and over,
like veins

it has never heard of the word bulb
yet from the dark earth
it pushes its heart ---

   as headdress,
   as opened light

a poet & two poppies

in the room where she sleeps,

past the mirrors and moons
of hours mute, morning finds her
with doves, filled with dawn

behind the curtains autumn
completes itself in a row
of poplars,

and against the window,

the bronze beginnings
of sunbirds and bells
that were stilled so long
by the night

ray by ray, the room
warms - two poppies

in a vase turn their heads
towards the day's slight-amber
pane

in her bed the warmth
of her body turns
to no one

jasmine

tonight,

    I pour my voice
    through your window....it wants
    nothing but to scent you with sighs

    of stars

a red hibiscus day

fire & grace

long i stood here

with my eyes; two black butterflies,
hunting realms where the winds have gone
for a glimpse of something, for words
and moments that have escaped
the gardens of my gaze

they came back
            with a red hibiscus

that, like a flamenco dancer,
unfurls its skirts in intimate cadences
of *fuego y gracia*, and flings
the pollen of its heart
far and wide. my eyes

lift and lift,
fly off to a day
when the pollen that erupted
from the center of our intimacy
rolled in waves to the ends of skins
and winds and stars –

it was as beautiful,
and as brief

jacaranda blues

nothing

    trumpets the heart's
delicate bruise colour

        bluer than a jacaranda
        ... in bloom

fleur de lotus

at dawn

    two stars surface
from hips of moon and mud -

    lush with light we are
sun, lily, water

african violets

they should ban African violets:

    those things bloom just a touch too purple
    on all the damn windows sills
    of sexual frustration

early spring

think of
me as spring coos
in dove vocals, and trees
blossom half-open flags against
the sky

(winter) rose

your body in the middle
of mine

       is a thrust
       of colour

my blood
understands:

a poinsettia, high
on its stalk,
rapt and red

- and winterless

fire lily

red word of beginning .. fire is her passion
~ Octavio Paz

your body on my body
is a grass fire made flesh

you open my skin with a rush of coals
from your mouth; a flame nests
in my belly, each breast
a bell of red words

legs leave me, spark east and west;
my name goes up in smoke:

a flower is born of your mouth

vignettes in frangipani

I

trees heavy with scent
hold the night up
with their hands,
and break

your scent in the dark hours

    I try to remember the glow
    of limbs, and your hands,
    frangipanis of light

II

thoughts of you are a whitish sound
of trembling, moons and moths
that keep hanging
as scarves for the wind

III

there comes a time when the sap slackens,
when summer turns fall, and I
every flower falling from the umbel
of your fingers:

an anthology of touch, undone
and un-gathered

IV

my hands now
are a scent through the night,
too slight to hold you

gift: more than one-day-pretty

I gave you more than the one-day-pretty
of morning glories fluttering
along a fence:

the reckless red of poppies that hovers
above spring, became yours too; the sudden
yellow of happiness, and jasmine stars,
too bright to flee the daylight

I write you every flying flower I am and was, also
those still at rest, and clap a paper net
over the butterflies of moments and years:

the small
and beautiful;
the immortal and beyond

even when on your fingertips the dust
of flight settled and died, and your hands
carry the forget-me-nots of my closed over wings

origami

in a dance of tongue and mouth
and hands, in creases and shapes
that only the body can read

we fold each other,
then fold again

over

    and over

till from the flat sheet of the bed
the petals of a flower begin
to stir,

and bursts

itself open in a straight-rising sigh
that scatters all the seeds
of inhibition

february in plum

every time as last winter
in plum blossoms
flutter

    ground wards

and the trees,

from deep within
their heartwood, laugh
against the white
of landscape
and eye

again, you fall
with your laughter
into the year rings
of my navel,

a flowering month
comes alive
    beneath
    my skin,

and my heart plums,
rose-red

when dandelions open & close

when I come to you....

wild geese fly low,
their feet trail a mass
of ruffling veils,
overflowing with storm

warm and blue-grey
and bluer and greyer still

the dust of continents
scents through the trees –
my garden breathes
deep in
         and out

a dandelion closes before
the coming rains,
a rustle of petals oils the air

(somewhere, softly a dove groans)

soon, I'll come flying to you,
overflowing with storm
and dream

like dandelion blossoms
in the promise of rain,
I'll close and open

with a dove soft-groaning
in my eyes

summer revisited

now leaves moor against my days
with their slow sails
of cinnamon and clove

I hear them fizz
on the porch: a paisley whirlwind,
a swirl of withered summers -

and while April falls from the branches,
while the mango of the sun wanes,
and clouds, like damask tablecloths
put out to dry, wave wavering
on the wind

I recover you from the spilled autumn
that smells like your skin,
sip your mouth of sangria
and kisses

and again, in my hair
grows the warm dahlia
of your hand

hours of flower and flame

as one
poet and poem,
pen and eye; yet only
a fragment of the self falls on
these lines

© Nicolette

from love's mouth

I came to know the vocabulary
that invented me:

it's the poetry
in universe, god in good
and his plan in the planets;

the gift in forgiveness,
and all the ways of gain
in always loving
again

it's the light for reading love
with my whole body

and the arm in warmth
that binds the *u* and *i*
in union

to lark

Alles van waarde is weerloos
- Lucebert

i know it too -

and furthermore the black
sparrows of loss,
pinned down
in the final chapter
of ink

through the thin night
the timid cantos
of women find me

we laugh and weep;
no other defense here

(and I remember Lucebert:
*everything of value
are defenseless*)

outside
the rain walks
around the house;
it brings some comfort

but the hour, the hour

is a deep corridor,
hung with the paused

selves of women
who dream

of Van Gogh's skylarks
rising from the rustle
of wheat fields

like water & light in my hand

in loving memory of my father, Arnold de Jager

at times it comes back -

in my palms I hold
the finch eggs
of your eyes,

and with fingers mute,
try to unweave you
from the wickerwork
of white-coated voices,
the flat horizons of heart
monitors and the grass
sting of death;

my hand hushed, and still
on your shoulder,
rooted in the silence
of the inexpressible:

call your brother and sisters

in the presence of shadows
I touched you in the sea
rippling out to the sun,
in the dust of the Little Karoo
clinging to your footsteps,
in the wind, blue and old,
and in the water and the light

in my hand

return to light

for my mother, Diane de Jager-
to the memory of my grandmother

I was too young to know

life is a dialogue
between spirit and dust,
tending, as all mouths do,
towards silence;

too young to fear
for our names, naked
and opened, balanced
on the edge of scalpels
and shards

how could I understand

that with the turn of a doorknob
you were already wind,
written with the initials
of the beyond,

and that I
would return to live
a child's life

by means of loss

when hadedahs laugh

monsters pitchfork
today with yesterday's
filth:

you fear
flames; so scared
I am of smoke

while we subscribe
our dreams
to funk,

love sits
on rooftops of morn,
sneering

in the ha-ha-ha
of hadedahs

the grey shawls of sacrifice

muffled sun
and the long arms
of palm trees wear a grey shawl --

like *la doncella.* in her grave, high
on Llullaillaco, fattened with fear,
frozen and far

from arms,

how her voice
must have tattooed
the rock walls with prayer:

come *cover-my-eyes-coca-leaf*
come *cradle-me-sea come*
close-me-mist

for everything she'd hoped
would ripen and swell
in the sun

were laid to rest one morning
under the grey shawl
of sacrifice

grammar of the heart

Shatter my heart so that a new room
can be created for limitless love
~ anon

simply two syllables
in shatter,
synonymous
with its verbal associates
destroy and undone

how strong it vibrates
in the blood;
no need here
for attributive adjectives
or the supplementary service
of auxiliaries

the tremor
of its final consonant
burrows into the walls
of the heart
till some cracks
open

and it razes and wrecks,
splinters doors and roofs –
the end result trills
in the rolled *r*
of ravaged

so shatter, shatter my heart

for the consequential alliteration
from ruin to a new
room

where love is made
a permanent
verb

scatterings

somewhere we have loved:

    so many lost stars
    turned leaf; fall
    as autumn. somewhere

    a wind will find
    what we have
    scattered; will start
    their wings;
    will give them

    back

to poem this piano

for Arnold

does not require Beethoven's breadth
of utterance, or Chopin's
evenness of touch

it does not mean hearing
an eruption of Vivaldi's
autumn leaves,

or Blue Danubes
filling empty spaces
with echoes and runs

to poem this broad wood
is simply to watch my son's hands
walking across a landscape of lost elephants,
until he too gets lost in the andante composition

of his own, private world

quicksilver

this is how dreams depart:

(with a fall of eyes,
dark, against the lime-
white laughter
of morn,

and feet, lapping
up their own scars
from the spilled shadows
of remembering

the smell of loss stretches
without pause; it resonates
in the lump in my throat,
and in branches -

already, tomorrow
jogs away with the road;

and there are only
the flaking fog and the trees:
pallbearers of broken
mirrors)

foiled and silver

poem for my heart

this poem for you,

my not-round word,
the colour of beginning and end;

unselfed verb of my breast,
my constant occupation,
wind-rose of passion,
dahlia of my scars

rest on me,
close all your senses,
leave your lips half-open:

for there is only your fire against so many cold things,
only your tenderness against arrows and stones
only your glance to uncloud the sun

to put myself away

On reading Ingrid Jonker

to put myself away
in a quiet sleep of lambs
and of seeds

put away
in the white flitting
of moths,

in the thorn-bush of memories,
in your drowned flame

to put myself away in my words

ever woman, ever growth

she's
    leaving
           the static
hours of this bed,
past's pillows and canes –
for she's woman, gentle
womb of breaths, navel of life;
ever movement, murmur of hip.
from shriveled song and sigh she rises
to where a new door opens ..... in the east

verse in largo

On reading Sylvia Plath's "Sheep in Fog"

Fog have wiped away the lights.
Families of Christmas trees
regard me silently,
I discomfort them.

A far-off train whistles
in silver.
Oh melancholic
horse the colour of distance,

hooves, breaking mirrors
in my breast –
all day this
day has been mourning.

A sore blossom looks on.
My bones murmur absence,
the largo verses of hills
melt my eyes.

They emphasize me
in a hinterland of cold
beds without arms,
a single slow eternity.

when all our doves leave us

meet me where nothing dies – zen koan

meet me with the face
you had before you were born,
for I'll recognize even the shadow
of your name on a plain of mist.

I, again, will break the bread
of light in your eyes, and simply be
chalice and wine. in your throat,
softly, a dove will groan - you

whose hands have tasted
little of the good earth
of a woman.

between us a flower will open,

and you'll understand how many
amaranthine moons
a single arum unfolds

from eve's diary

I am not an afterthought;

I don't journey through this world dressed as a broom
or a recycled rib in whore stockings
seeking evil, seeking tongues,
the mouths of dead men
and snakes,

and I no longer carry the patriarchal cross
of unappled wood

I am *ha-'adama*, the shape
of *ha-'adams's* longing
– we are the source
of each other

I happen to like being hip-
swaying woman,

the fruit of knowledge,
the gentle word that passes
between Adam's blood
and mine;

mother of earth and water,
of seeds and bones and bells,
the uterine flower is mine
and the circle of milk;

my body opens
into life after life

I am not an afterthought;
I'm a culmination

footnotes from a mother

for Barend, Diane & Arnold

although mother is just a simple word
I was not really prepared for this task;
I only had the classroom
of my heart

and the acquired knowledge
that life teaches through opposites:

at times a slither of light,
other times full moons

(always the word *child* floats on my thoughts)

sometimes I still hold you as a baby tight,
other days spell your name
like birds in a flock
        and the whole, open sky

wherever your eyes fly   I am there
in the shade of your lashes

and when your eyes return to their hollows
with perceptions of joy
or sorrow, my eyes too are crying
on your cheek

when your wings complain against the black rain,
the one syllable of my love
will carry you towards the sun

I am the warmth that follows
in the wake of your breath
and every wind bears the scent of my caress

whenever I speak your name seven moons appear
from night; I am equal to thousands of stars,
naked and young,

and my heart sleeps full of peace
like dust beneath a tree

sing

the time will come
when i will unravel my song
from the accompaniment
of scars and sob.

i will love again
the stranger in my own arms,
the one who was my self,
who knows the sonority
of my voice by heart,
and say:

sit with me here.
sing.

and when I close my eyes

and when I close my eyes
lightly,

I see
the Ganges flow into the Nile:
you and I, old as tears,
washed loose from the silt of suffering
to retake the highlands where,
from the dark earth,
as lotuses we arise

and when I close my eyes
tightly,
I see for what
my heart broke horizons

promise you'll never think of me

promise you'll never think of me
in statue terms -

i don't want to see myself
sculpted in your thoughts,
hair marbled with bird shit

and with a body that allowed
no access to its interior

      space

your name in my mouth

...love, with its magic rays,
opened my eyes, and
brushed my soul
with its fingers
of fire.

© *Kahlil Gibran*

in the saffron of our laughter

moshka bokkie

saffron hour
and a light breaks
from the sea

in your room
somewhere between bamboo blinds
and a bed spiced with bodies - two words,
your laughter and the morning
sudden and red
like a ladybird

dropped on my belly

at peggy's cove

Nova Scotia

'twas cold –-

over the sea the wind
rolled up a flock
of gulls, a Pleiades
of living stars

on one big wing
a whole constellation
moved light houses
in me

when you
signed my name
in the warm guest book
of your arms

winter fled
without a look of feet

knowledge

I will die kissing your crazy old mouth -
Sonnet XCIII, 100 Love Sonnets by Pablo Neruda

love in a narrow bed,
the lamp still burning
when the first bird song stirs the curtain,
and Neruda's *Cien sonetos de amor* kept open
at *I will die kissing your crazy old mouth*
proclaiming, that through us,

the earth will continue to live

blue pause

there was a murmur of waves
breaking; you opened -

your mouth
filled with water, your eyes
two drops of blue salt
dipped into my breasts

that morning in your bed
the world changed;

our language was in pieces,
we were broken words
brought to blueness,

names suspended
in the pause of a duvet:

our only scape of sky

berceuse

berceuse, Chopin

too yellow loss exposed itself
in the birth of that day; we split
with our voices into tears, open

and free. I loved you
the most then,

because in the very sun
that broke us

apart,

was the discovery
of me in you

how i see you

guest poem by Steve Melvin (aka quietly burning, 2007)

you say
  you know the way
i see you

(but ... how could you?)

i say
  if ever
    there's a day
     you wake
         to realize
         as i do
     that a sky
   can never make
its own moon

(all I need is ... is you!)

then you can say
 you know the way
i see you

to pour myself as moon

in response to quietly burning's "how I see you", 2007

around so much earth I've circled,
seeking a sky. here I float now into the time zone
of your glance --

for you I want to be moon; to pour myself
through the winter branches of your thoughts, through
the nebula that slows your eyes, and your feet,
devoid of sight

open your windows to the fullness of my glow,
so that you hear the leaves of my flower
ripple on the wind; feel my heart where it grows
against the panes

let me moon through you; in you
I found my sky

touch, almost

an ostrich feather,
its head turned sideways
against the light,

makes my hand remember -

thoughts follow fingers
up a long, white stairway,
intimately plumed
in sleep

   hesitate
            hesitate

on the brink of your brow,
as if again, lightly, I brush
the fringe from your eyes

# of all my soft blue days

of all my soft blue days
I only want to write your eyes;
so that I can feel the warm breasts
of doves beating against my palms,
and that I, when I want to,
later can read of a soft blue
day and of you, always
you here with me

ache

here are the house
the room   the window

shadows slither down walls
inure to the still-born; the water
that weeps in the pipes

the ceiling listens
to the lamentations of wind
and branch;   to whatever
vilifies the mercurial
rhythms of rapture

the window aches - in vain
its darkened eyes try to ostracize
the leafless rain, its liquid
trains of thorns

here I wait for you
to alleviate the void - this sad
house   this room   this window -

with the magnanimity
of skin against skin, the birth
of two shadows on rapturous walls,
your blood that sings in my pipes

till then
my house aches

wind

when green the wind
untangles the branches
I recall my hair –

how dark it had blown against
the Mt Fuji of your pillows

at 5:30 am

all the songs that we've made -

    wagtail in from the trees,
    lark in vertical notes
    through slightly-parted
    curtains -

    waking up, I thought
    it a honeyeater
    out-caroling
    the blackbirds
    of sleep

    but it's only the 5:30 sky
    bluebirding your eyes

are always with me

i hold your name in my mouth

bokkie buoy

the moon empties, the moon fills
and so many words break
their own promises,
turnabout and turn
winter

but your name in my mouth
is the pinkish tinge
of warmth

my tongue meets
anew each day

eyes of the poet

it's winter in my room
the white bed   the faded curtains

the floor covered with books
and paper   paper   paper,
whispers

of forgotten poems,
dried flowers of faraway seasons

the night has taken root –
an infinite palette of dark hues
like a deep blue flower

in my winter room I listen
to the night wind
unbuttoning the clouds,

throwing water stars,
blue-tinted florets,
against the window

they shine like eyes,
carrying the scent of mountains
and fields

there's no light on in my room
but tonight I can write again:

I only need the nocturnal blue
cornflowers of raindrops -

oeillets du poete: small eyes of the poet
to write the season of your eyes

over the bed   the curtains   the floor

whisper

into the pool of my ear, a word drops slowly:
a shadow of sound, a single drop,
a ripple from the red conversation
of your lips

it falls and breaks and spreads its water -
soft of syllable and resonance it trickles
down my hair, and within me
my heart listens

time and again,

it is this passage of temperature, this sipping
of intimate breath, this undertone
of fluttering flags that susurrates
an upsurge of doves

from my breast

at 6:00 am

Cape Town, South Africa

the day falls open in your voice
                in a language of amethyst

table mountain imitates you,
the city looks at me with your eyes

my soul's wet with morning
                and the smoke-blue texture of your voice

at 6.00 am I become a murmuring water-mirror
                wherein all the species of tomorrows awake

and like the aromatic trees

and like the aromatic trees
of Tamil Nadu,

you and I, dear,
achieved our oil content;
the anxiety
of dark heart woods
uprooted, distilled
into sweet
              scents of
                        sandalwood

this viscous yellow tinge
persists
(at last)

(o
    o
      z
        e
          s

through pores a tremble
of breath, a rhythm
of sighing rainy seasons)

so floatingly-fragrant
      the fruition of fingers
(and lips and voice
and thighs),

and the core-deep
in-
cen(se)-
sing (of trees)

       and us

the madness

Cuando amor no es locura, no es amor.
When love is not madness, it is not love.
~ Spanish Proverb

I've been a whisper
of wholeness

wilted, Janis Ian and I
talked to God, dialed a prayer,
while mr Cohen climbed mountainsides
to wash our eyelids in the rain – so long,
so long!

before today my body was
toneless

now it tears off its own ears
and runs with them to your lips,
crazy sunflowers on the canvas
of your tongue (sigh)
I know, Van Gogh
– madness!

once it was a glass vase,
quite opaque,

empty of long-stemmed colours
drinking its liquid murmur
but you permeated her, cleared
her - some days there are
more flowers her vase can hold

- she's been gleamed

my nerves are tuned, my veins
resonate

with perpetual motion, the full moon
appears with your face, I howl (often)
you did this, pure genius at work
darling, the straight jacket
of your arms my only
asylum

pianissimo

your fingertips
across my skin

a leaf
falls,

    see-

        saws

    down
    through the air

into the small of my back
your hand pours
the softest sound

new dress

on the bedroom floor
a gathering of empty
clothes --

in the sleeves
of your arms
and the soft texture
of your voice

your body becomes
my new dress:

slowly it gives back
the warmth that I've lost
to the floor

flame

10 May 2006

you are in me
all flamed seasons:

your mouth
hangs wild berry sighs
on my summers;
all our yellow moments
autumn leaf
through me -

see how I rustle
in your hand
of hearths and hue

a bite out of the moon

*If anyone asks you
how the perfect satisfaction
of all our sexual wanting
will look, lift your face
and say, like this:*

~ Rumi

morning comes in amber

morning comes with a bed
where, like two hand-rolled
cigarettes, we awake

it comes with an ember
in the body, with an outpour
of flames, while snow
falls outside

you scent through me
with a voice of smoke
and ochre;

I float on your tongue
like hand-picked aromas
of *café de manha*

like this,
I want morning to find us:

with its bed,
its flames and happy skins
on sheets where,

like melted flowers,
the amber accents of our love
coalesce,

and we glow,
we glow

gingered

in the attention of your mouth
I open skywise;

    a fountain of red words
    bursts out from within,
    rises,
        falls,
            scatters itself
in a surge of exclamations;

    gingered on the stalk
    of your tongue
    I weigh no more
                than a ripple

naked nights

the night is enormous
and this skin is as desolate
as the *r* in winter

this body who is woman;
exposed flesh of love,
unfolded star of hips,
flower of your stem,
invention of your hands
and your mouth; once
trace of your body -

now naked wish,
longing for consolation

para siempre

A star shone at the hour of our meeting.
~ J.R.R. Tolkien

you happened to my body,
and I feel

a star

opening in me –
unnamed; perhaps a new
polaris,

la superba, sol, comet
with your scent and touch.
I fall over the horizon
of the bed,

so undirected

between linen
and ceiling, the jasmine
of our hips, bruised
with sighs that shine

siempre
siempre

you pin me to eternity
with a single star

and I feel

chanson

your hands
are a wine-press:

when you hold me, I hear
the passionate purple laughter
of grapes

beached

your mouth blows on my heart,
near the sea, at the edge of
my foaming breasts

the moist flames of your tongue
spread through my naked blood,
echo in my red depths

with the sound of foghorns,
sea birds and bells
in the midst of wind

until the wavering waters
of my sea shiver and splinter
against the flaming coast
of your lips

dunes

wind blue,
your eyes break the day,
unlock my silence
from the dark
dew

and I
become desert, further
than the eyes can drink,

more naked
than the dunes
repeating my breasts

fire damage

with mouth and hand I unlatch you,
suck you in to the ceiling
of my hips

in spurts of lubricated moans we unfold
our walls; you burn through
my shadow, I spill
from your name

so unpoetically jumbled
we call our sigh

till I'm only a brass stain
on your doorknob, and you

hinge-hinge
upon your every frame

alliteration(s)

(for you, because you)

scribe me with verses,
letters and spaces
in your eyes, naked
synonyms

of smouldering syllables,
shivering in scintillating
stanzas

alliteration ripples
my skin, my body

simmers in metaphors
of exclamations,
hips stutter
asterisks

the rhyme of breaths,
styled in assonance,
staggers beyond
the synopsis of
syntax -

Solomon sighs
in full sentences...

I fall asleep
in his song

a vermilion hour

the day steps out
of the diurnal shades
of innocence into sunset's
liquid red key of C

dusk smoulders on the horizon
in variable colors of flying
Persian carpets - sensuous
and warm

synonyms of sun and mars
pool in the glass bowl
on the table – marigold,
poinsettia, fire-lily –

it is as if Vermeer himself
has poured me a glass of wine
from his palette
of passion

and brushed my vivid
red streams with
the fervent fingers
of fire -

deep, around the root
of my spine, sunset wraps
itself in low vibrations
of desire

here, where I await you
in the definitions of
a vermilion hour

we are so much lighter now

for years we've walked
with buried hips, entombed
by so much cold time

in the absence of shivers and stars,
they have forgotten how to glow,
how to leak long rivers -

and then love: the single syllable
that pours open a thousand tunnels,
returned our hips from the earth,

scooped us up with its deep spoons
until our faces blurred
against the stars

a lighter weight

night comes down
with its shadows
and its clarities;

in my window
a round dove
swells with light –

without saying a word
she nests in my belly
with the whiteness
of another vertical
hour

when toes and shrieks
leapt skyward,
shattering
the calm course
of a star,

and the sofa,
stored with worlds
and waters
of waxing truths,

weighed less
than fugitive words
like moon,

       and love

anchored

oceans
sing through my hips,
flurries billow your blood;

intimately anchored, we ride
the storm

daily bread

of all the breads my hands have eaten,
I choose only the white creation
of your skin

your body defines earth's gifts
to my nose – I am surrounded

by yellow scents of wheat fields,
the blue breezes of wild sage and cornflower
and the nomadic aroma of rain
weaving its tongue around stalks of sun

only in the attention of your skin I live,
filled with a fragrance of seasoned kitchens
and fires, of herb butter and the yeast
of flesh on flesh

and my hands and my mouth
and everything that once were
scentless, without spice,
without zest

now keep breathing, keep absorbing
the deep savour that you bring,
the high climate of your breast,

keep folding and folding themselves
around the steamy tower of manna
that is you

far, above

one morning your eyes
open – so soft so wide
the sun hangs out a fragrance
of love (I fall from
your orange tree voice)
in blossoms wild and white
I know your body sweet-
heart like night the stars
now warm and dim
(like you) sometimes life
becomes so good
graciously good:

one morning love the hour
unfolds the body awakes with
a bird's-eye view of itself

to cloud the sun

I started to dress for goodbye —

    your eyes, a plea:
    I'm not done with you yet

    I wanted to stay on the bridge
    of your foot, or perhaps kneel
    and become slave choirs,
    my body a chant in the cathedral
    of your hands;

    that morning in your room I did

    turn my back like a cloud
    on the sun that threatened
    to burn the bridge to *not yet*

vibrato

this very moment,
you and I here –

moment of metamorphosis,
of passion fastening to our bodies,
moment that is
yours and mine –

     my eyes dark with the dark
     primitive hypnosis
     wherein faraway landscapes drift;
     your body is crystal and tumbles
     like stars into the hollow
     of my name

here we are, here is all
we need:

two inner-worlds that fold into one
in a vibrato that binds and binds

on reading cummings

somewhere i have never traveled ~ E E Cummings

i see doves rise from an old pear tree
and hang (deep blue grapes)
on the high pergola of the moon.
i smile, knowing that my body with your body
is somewhere i have traveled, gladly beyond
all pear tree restrictions

not even the doves know such moonfulness

tambourine

rhythmic
against my hips
the warm jingle jangle

of yours

leaves and longing

in the center of the earth
I shall push aside the emeralds
so that I can see you —

~ Pablo Neruda

facing a new day

Forgetting someone is like forgetting to turn off the light in the
backyard so it stays lit all the next day. But then it is the light that
makes you remember.
~ Yehuda Amichai

I lean my eyes
against the day's
sharp-white
pane

just sun, unjust sun -

it grows everywhere,
and in my throat
my voice bows

because
        the silence
                    between us

is taller
than a scream,

and as precise
as the image of the sun

crushing
the morning star

i miss you like the leaves

today

is a slow autumn; I
keep falling

  through

evergreen pines
of separation

like wind through a flute

another winter's night. somewhere
from my insides a moan
slips. so clumsily,
I call your name.

I, who only wanted to lay my voice
against your mouth, in the lasting
orgasm of your breath,

softer, drowsier than wind
through a flute,

sit with the thin notes of silence,
abandoned by the song,

and my voice, I see, is something
that keeps slipping past
your mouth

weighted

we stand in the winter sadness
of startled leaves,
our voices blank of sound,
the arms brittle
and bare

if only I could lay my hand
on your hand
and with my mouth
against yours
say —

something

like wind
pouring summer through leaves

but winter keeps falling,
and leaf by leaf,
my branches

give way

slow lament

dark eyes slender
into drops ---

spread their water
and their salt
with sad insistence
like slow white snails

here my voice stumbles

Here I love you ~ Pablo Neruda

Here my voice stumbles.
Through the pale arms of trees
the wind pours itself.
Against the window the moon skirls
its silver solitude.
The grass is wet of dreams.

Night unfurls in dark carnations.
A white moth falls from the Southern Cross.
Sometimes a wing. Far far water stars.
Oh, the hoarse cry of a lighthouse.
Alone.

The dark is never silent; even my eyes are noisy.
Somewhere a black sea echoes and re-echoes.
The bay is big.
Here my voice stumbles.

Here my voice stumbles; the horizon hides you in vain.
I love you still among these cold things.
Sometimes my words leave me like birds of passage
winging towards endless summers.
I see them flying off in flocks of ink.

The piers sadden when dusk moors here.
My tongue grows quiet, moist to no purpose.
My longing wrestles with the starry distances,
but time and sand stifles my mouth.

The moon cries at every window.
The grass is full of night and water.
And as I love you, my voice stumbles
over a single branch and a paled dream.

quartered

Inspired by Salvador Dali's "Melting Soft Watch"

this too yellow afternoon
handcuffs me

all day
quarters of the hours
have been torturing me

wishing bones of longing
spiral the wounded hours
past themselves

everywhere   I search   for you

the hushed, tremulous sound
of my locked wrists
travels the landscape

of your body
on crutches of dream

I'm stuck   at the unsettling hour   of you

only the blue horizon tries
to recover
the natural cycle

of sunrises and sunsets

opened

On reading Sylvia Plath's "Jilted"

My thoughts are wind and stone,
startling the window -
fossilized tears bemoan
your absence at my elbow.

Tonight a single branch, dear
howls blue and long,
and I bow to the viscous veneer
of its concentrated song,

while like a dark carnation,
musky, petals apart,
throbs inflamed and swollen
my ripe, full-open heart.

a lesson in winter

Halifax Airport, February 2006

it was black, the day of suitcases and snow;
red, the screams of road signs -
turn around, wrong way – that broke
the meter of voice and eye

in the long tunnel to too far,
before the plane stirred snowflakes
and stars, and a wind sock swelled
with separation,

I turned around;

my mouth went like a wave, discharging
into yours a flurry of kisses –
you caught them all, you said,
before two continents slipped
in between tomorrows and lips

I remember love
was everything they said it would be;
but love forgot to make me too blind

to see I wasn't one of my own kisses

lost echo

Each night I cut out my heart,
in the morning it would grow again...
~ Michael Ondaatje

winter crawls up trees,
lies grim on branch and leaf;
even my words have become thin

between my lips and your ears
something goes dying.
something with the exquisite yellowness
of poppies, something of sorrow
and oblivion

you are so far,
and my voice does not touch you;
my words cross your heart
without stopping

you have hidden yourself
and leave me to separate your face
from the lament of my mouth,
and from cold things

tonight I'll cut out my heart
(it's the only word here
that is warm and swollen)

and remember you as you were
before the word love
lost its echo

when words escape

how does one voice forget
when still,

    like water over sand,
    you cling to my body's glow,
    and against the breakwater
    of my throat the firm trump of

    the sea?

to window

and I wanted my eyes to be
your window;

not the stained-glass of cathedrals
through which weak light falls,
but the uncurtained
circle-flight of a bay window
for your heart to drink
from God's hand

(yes, also the salty taste of the sea),

it is the same —
the way migrant birds know
the horizon is not the end
of the world;
the way they believe in their wings
that summer is never
too far -

but even the three panoramas
of faith, hope and love
could not window you a view;

my eyes now only pieces of glass
thrown into the water,
where again it will turn
to sand

too white the day

let us label this morning
ornate-white

even the interview
between early sun and glass
is a liturgy in magnolia
and alabaster

only kohl lines of trees - dark
as foreshadows of separation -
rescind the still life
of snow and air

word still we hold each other
in the iridescent nudity
of tears and winter
at the window

the hours
of our quota togetherness
have run dry now - and fingers
hips and red forces in blood
and bone

become a desperate viaduct
over the too white
presence

of goodbye

between your thoughts & your hands

on reading Piet de Jager

when night comes down

with its weight of crows
and all that caw me
to non-being,

my head still rests
on your lap
where I left it someday –

between

your thoughts
and your hands
and everything
that remain
unfinished for us;

and I wonder
if at times you see
how visible the silence,

and when it's alone,
how cold a moan
becomes

september poem

And then you came and reveal yourself in all that you are.
And then you came and read me where I have never hoped
to be read. Not in this life.
~ Taja Kramberger

I

long before the Canada geese
of your voice cried your love
through me at Heathrow,

and carried me south
through many spaces of sky.

I knew you loved me

II

now that the birds
are returning with the blue
eyes of September

and the sound of spring
is stirring on every branch

I put a few feathers
in my vase of hours, for yo
and I in those days,

and for the migrant birds
of love whose feathers were born
with us and winged
our hearts

III

I lift my breasts, inhale and exhale
the scent of spring, knowing
that once upon a September

you called
my name

and I was half undone with joy,
just like the branches
and the birds

seasons

perhaps one summer's day you'll rise
from our bed, gazing over a garden
full of birds and whistle

perhaps you'll wonder about last year's snow
or the apple blossoms that have fallen
in orchards across the road

perhaps you'll rub your hands together
to wipe away the small secret letters
that I've written there

   they will come back
   like the blossoms and the birds

when at night you embrace nothing

how do you think me then:

moon-naked, adrift
on your body's many seas,

> or do I stay
> moored to the black
> quay of your long long sleep?

wind sleeve

at the end of each runway a mouth trembles
with wind; its cheeks cone the blue
tongue skirling of eyes and air
and accumulated
separations

cluster of bright beads

*It is in the shelter of each other
that the people live.*

~ Irish Proverb

to a child

The ring of your mouth is a beautiful joy.
I want to fill it with parrots and song,
the circus of the brave
whose laughter you dream -
tambourine, chimpanzee,
little

flute of a reed,
flower cup in which music
should be grand and clear.

Not these chilblained lips
of discouragement, this
broken circle without a voice.

voiceless

Silence kills Africa's children

and it's not the shadow,
the dark wing of death,
that lowers my soul
to elbows
and dust

it is the black-clad silence,
the blood-stained absence
of hands,

the tongues without fingers,
without throat,
without sound

there is no one here,
but some hoof prints, no one
but the dormant drums
of stones and straw

there is no one here,
but the stagnant stench
of ignorance

waiting for a poem

Mossel Bay, 2007

I dip my eyes into the silence
of a winter's day; how blue
the sun in Africa

seagulls call a few pencil strokes
against the sky, vaguely-white
as the morning moon,

  and there
  it is: in the mist

awakening on the dunes,
in the silver mussel of the sea,
and on the window sill

and against the leafless light,
in a mantis' endless green
prayer

paternoster

West Coast, South Africa

here mews break open the blue air
with brushstrokes of bamboo
and buoy —

and I walk myself out of time;
past days of long lists, away
from the cold workings
of clocks

it's only me, and my toes, deep
in seashells and salt,
losing ourselves
where the morning makes water
in the navel of the bay

down the coast, an elephant
humps itself in the embrace of waves;
its stone trumpet, like a foghorn,
sniffing the wind for prayers
of fishermen and flares

with my eyes I gather in Africa's grace
where fishing boats grow on the sand
in rosaries of flaking wood,
and the houses, foamy-white,
nap on the brow of boulders

like this, with mews
writing amen against blue,

I want to walk with you,
with my shadow disappearing
in yours

Paternoster: "our father"

siyabona africa!

beautiful

the orange notes
of sun rising
from the camel thorns,
warm shadows
of dawn; gemsbok hooves
on the shimmering drums
        of dunes -

the Kalahari unfolds
her hand in the sounds of colour:
orange-red, quivering blue
horizons, bushman
grass and cheetah,
a windblown finger of land

oh, wild song of the wind,
sing me north   deeper
on the roar
of lions and sands   further
as the marabou's black wings

to where the chorus line
of water kudu
and the dream ships
of elephant and hippo
ripple the stillness
of a water
wilderness:

Chobe, Okavango

oh, *ilizwe elihle* *
let my eyes inform my soul:

Siyabona Africa: we see Africa!

* ilizwe elihle: Xhosa for "beautiful world"

ring of roses

if I could gather days
of crayons and clay in my hand
if I could shape fresh
doves in your sleep,
I would do it for your face
of poppies and bells
and for the light of milk
that flows from your mouth

because when you're alienated,
when your veins swell with fear,
rivers become quiet,
mountains go grey overnight,
trees hang out black cloths at noon
and the sun falls wounded
in its own shadow

but when you're loved whole
and breathe kindness and joy,
rivers sing of new roses,
mountains are born again,
stars of hope bud on the branches of trees
and the sun dances ring-a-ring-a-rosies
with a peacock feather in its hat

namib

endlessly wide
the sand grows; how fearless
your stare of solitude

nothing moves -
only the sun takes place
with its yellow teeth

and thin-blue days,
blowing your secret
from dune to dune,
beyond horizons of eyes
and understanding

place of great plains,
of silence and skeleton,
of waterless waves
and welwitschia,

I wanted to invade you
with words, trample you
to poem

but you make me watch
with lips detained
by thirst,
with feet heavy
and red of fatigue,

and this poem: mere mirage

wolanani

we embrace each other

child,
little cluster
of bright beads,

there are still arms
that gather warmth,
heart-drums in this land
of Africa that lift your chin
to the sun

and there are hands
that spread hope,
fingers that rebuild
the huts of new memories
and skins that hum
music back into your mouth

little one,
here in the village of arms
begins the renaissance
of your youth, your happiness,
the drawing of your circle
of courage

and there, from the black
beads of your eyes,
once wounded by blood,
will again unfold
all the flags
of the rainbow

nightfall

Buffelsdrift, Oudtshoorn

the hour
          changes colour –
quietly the day stirs,
withdraws from the hills.... and there, night
comes in

birds leave
in a handful of shadows..... deep
in flower bells the day's
                    aroma falls
                              asleep

south africa: the long walk

Inspired by the life story of Nelson Mandela (Madiba)

here lies the land of interrupted rhythm;
so many funeral events, so much earth,
so much waters dark
with laments

from the rubber bullets of apartness,
from cemeteries of vomited unity
and bones, the smoke of a sad republic
lifts towards where there is nothing
but separation

it's the sound of suppression, the bloody black
syllables of colour classification,
the weeping and sobbing
of segregated skins
in unhappy clothes

you hear it in the streets, the farewells in the mines,
in throats necklaced to death,
in pass books in hands,
the fists squirting fury
in spurts

it's eyes have died of severed dignity and roots
- they are two holes of bitterness
dying inwards; it has no youth;
only a long rumble of god-
forsakenness

if only someone would come from the islands,

from the mountains of good hope,
with the siren of freedom on his voice,
the roll call of peace in his gaze,
if only someone's knees
would pray:

Nkosi Sikelel' iAfrica: God bless Africa

here be dragons

Hier is inderdaad drake ~ Ilze van Staden

here are indeed dragons:

here in our houses and hearths;
in our happy homes
where children twitch and starve
in skins of sorrow and shame
and their toes gather the dust
of fear in the dark

here in the kingdoms we call ours,
between playgrounds, tea cups and tv
warm breaths swallow up little birds
of laughter, and childhoods,
like lobsters, are sentenced
to death alive

here where our children play
with marbles and dolls
here are
dragons

small protest

something
of me - I, will
live on in sparrow bones
of words: my small, white song against
demise

living words

taken
from the dark blood
and passed through my senses,
words grow hands and tongues, continue
to breathe

a poet

slides hand-carved schooners
through the thin neck of imagination

for the voyage
        beyond glass

about the author

Nicolette M van der Walt, whose first language is Afrikaans, grew up on an ostrich farm near Oudtshoorn in the Little Karoo region of South Africa. She has a masters degree in social work, obtained from the Nelson Mandela Metropolitan University, South Africa (bachelors degree obtained from Stellenbosch University). Her master's thesis was on the impact of the Mossgas Project (now PetroSA) on social issues in Mossel Bay and environs – the first of such studies in South Africa. She is the author of more than 25 professional manuals, programs and research papers relating to various aspects of social work. Nicolette also wrote the script for six educational films about child protection and HIV/Aids for pre-school children and their caregivers: Wolanani – We embrace each other (produced by Jchiannie Productions, South Africa), and was actively involved in the filming, directing and editing of these films. She is currently the Manager: Transformation & Development of the ACVV, one of South Africa's biggest welfare organizations. She is a lover of love, children, animals, poetry, sport, reading, nature and music and has been awarded for community work – both as a professional and as a volunteer.

She considers her writing to be influenced by the works of Pablo Neruda, Octavio Paz, Rumi, Kahlil Gibran, Ingrid Jonker, Antjie Krog and a wide variety of other international and South African poets. Nicolette currently lives with her family in Mossel Bay on the Garden Route in the Western Cape province of South Africa.

www.ingramcontent.com/pod-product-compliance
Lightning Source LLC
Chambersburg PA
CBHW021005090426
42738CB00007B/667